THE LIE OF THE LAND

Elaine Gaston

Doire Press

First published in July 2015

Doire Press
Aille, Inverin
Co. Galway
www.doirepress.com

Layout & cover design: Lisa Frank
Author photo: Hayley Madden
Cover image: *Low Road* by Elizabeth Magill
oil on canvas, 51 x 46 cm, 2013
(courtesy of Wilkinson Gallery, London)
www.elizabethmagill.com

Printed by Clódóirí CL
Casla, Co. na Gaillimhe

ISBN 978-1-907682-38-4

We gratefully acknowledge the assistance of The Arts Council of Northern Ireland.

LOTTERY FUNDED

ACKNOWLEDGEMENTS

Acknowledgements are due to the editors of the following in which versions of some of these poems appeared: *Poetry Ireland Review*; *Verse*; *The North*; *New Welsh Review*; *The Rialto*; *Buzz*, Templar Poetry; *Black Mountain Review*; *Study Ireland, Poetry*, BBC Two Northern Ireland; *National Poetry Competition 2013*, The Poetry Society; *Word of Mouth*, Blackstaff Press; *The Honest Ulsterman*; *Brangle*; *Life and Movement,* South Eastern and Social Care Trust; *re-COLLECT-ing*, Queen's University, Belfast/Naughton Gallery; *Manchester Open Poetry Competition*. Some of these poems have been recorded for the Seamus Heaney Centre Digital Archive.

I am grateful to the Arts Council of Northern Ireland for awards in the Artists' Career Enhancement Scheme 2014-15 and in the Support for the Individual Artist Programme, 2006 and 2008, which enabled me to work on this collection.

Heartfelt thanks to Dr Sinéad Morrissey and Dr Medbh McGuckian at the Seamus Heaney Centre for Poetry, Queen's University, Belfast; Cherry Smyth for reading; Elizabeth Magill; Linda France; Anne-Marie Fyfe; Judith Palmer at the Poetry Society; Lisa Frank and John Walsh at Doire Press; Damian Smyth at the Arts Council of Northern Ireland; Alastair Cooke; Robert Peake; Joan Newmann; Kate Newmann; Word of Mouth and Ballycastle Library.

Love and special thanks to my family and friends and all my teachers. I.m. Maureen Gaston and Kathryn Gaston who were there at the beginning.

CONTENTS

Early Map   9

Push-Bike   10

After Blackberry-Picking   11

Dunseverick   12

Portballintrae   13

The Bread Man   14

The Vegetable Man   15

The Library Van   16

Mother's Day   17

Lizzie Remembers the Persian Rug   18

What Would Jesus Say?   19

Letting it Draw   20

My Father Explains the Universe   21

New Year's Day   22

Offering   24

For the Whole Drive Across Buenos Aires   25

Open a Wardrobe   28

Keeping in Touch   29

Just Enough   30

Storm Damage   31

The Lump of Ailsa Craig   34

Donegal   35

The Lie of the Land   36

Rare Grooves   37

Night in Twinbrook   40

Jayne Cortez and The Firespitters at the Old Museum 42

Cycling Home from the Rotterdam Bar   43

Plastic Bullet   44

Getting to Chartres (During Peace Talks Back Home)   46

She Threw it Right into the Middle of the Garry Bog 48

Middle Months   49

Afternoon Mudra   50

Crow Glen, Belfast Hills   51

Fine Green Beans   52

My Russian Hat   53

Unmarked   54

Flashback   55

Living History   56

A Musician's Tale   57

Departure Lounge Heathrow to Belfast   59

Café   60

Daylighgin   62

I Text Myself Before Bedtime   65

Eóin's Last Day at School   67

The Eel on the Farm   68

Seasoned   69

Snowfall   70

Road, Glen, Island, Ocean   71

Old Croagh Woman   72

Rushes, Port Na Cailleach on St Brigid's Day   73

Walking to Marconi's   74

Notes   76

About the Author   79

For my mother and father,
Maureen and Joe,
with love and gratitude

Early Map
after John Hewitt

I know my way by the mossy stone,
the boggy field, the fairy thorn,
the house with the old milk churn stand,
the house which hides the bogeyman,

the cross where the brae meets Kilmoyle,
The Lazy Bends, The Arch, the school.
Names I was raised with slip down
like buttermilk and fresh-baked wheaten.

The mountain behind, the Antrim plateau
make their own picture, our window
the frame. Townlands stretch to the east
and the west, the north and the south of us,

shining basalt in my mind,
falling water through my hands,
ripe blackberries on my tongue:
Drumtullagh, Dunseverick, Lisnagunogue.

Push-Bike

She wrapped a tea-towel around buns or a brack,
packed sandwiches into a bread-bag
and strapped me into the seat on the back.

I pressed against her, arms around her waist,
her strong swimmer's legs pushing us up the brae
(legs that had saved a child from a whirlpool one day

in Donegal). Long grasses, cow parsley
crowded us as she worked and swayed
and sang, 'then up she goes to Antonio

with his ice cream cart'; on evenings in summer
we called with neighbours,
Annie's sick brother, Jamesy's mother.

One August evening, daylight almost gone,
she clicked the dynamo on, I heard its secret song,
'up we go, up we go, oh Antonio',

the lamp flickered in time with the pedals
when she stood up in the saddle for the hill.
Down the other side it was all freewheel,

midges, swallows, hedges flitted past
till we spun faster, faster,
her blowing hair and laughter

were all a blur,
as the warm air and wheels' whirr
lulled me to sleep against her constant back.

After Blackberry-Picking

She found last year's pots at the back of the cupboard,
set us to rinsing them in the scullery,
then put them in the oven to warm.
We picked over the fruit for leaves and worms,
helped to tip the berries onto the scales,
'That's six pounds, well done, that gives twelve in all.'
We watched them fall into the preserving pan,
poured tumblers of water, sugar in mounds
to swirl in a purple ocean. Berry islands
bobbed and frothed, simmered for hours
until a glob hardened on a cold saucer
and we knew the jam was set. Timing was all.
Too long and it could go past itself.
Once we had blackberry syrup with custard
all winter. She poured the hot mass into kilners,
we squabbled over who placed the waxed seal,
the rubber band, the cellophane circle.
My sister's good handwriting signed off each jar:
Blackberry Jam, 1lb, the month, the year.

Dunseverick

On hot days she packed a picnic after school,
crammed us all into the clapped-out Consul
and drove to the coast where big flat rocks
held the day's heat. We changed into swim-togs,
spread out the rug, lashed on *Ambre Solaire*,
then dared each other – the first swim of the year.
We splashed and charged and roared into the water,
came out mottled, numb; she squeezed dry our hair,
wrapped us in towels, shoved on windcheaters,
gave us hunks of wheaten slapped together
with a wedge of Edmund Black's good cheddar
gone sweaty in the sun. We crowded round her,
drank lukewarm orange from a plastic cup,
shared out a melting bar of *Fruit and Nut*.

Portballintrae

It's a faded Polaroid photo in my mind,
the steep slope down to the harbour wall,
me in gutties, cotton skirt, aertex shirt;

a diver breaking through the water
smooth as a seal, handing over a pouch.
An oilskin laid out like a table-cloth,

a man in shorts hunkered over the haul,
smoking *Gitanes*, speaking in French.
I sat on an upturned boat

– the smell of diesel and paintwork in the sun –
heard rumours of treasure,
galleon ships lost years before,

names like rubies in my head:
Port na Spania, Girona, Armada.

The Bread Man

Willie Scullion wore a winter hat
shaped like a Brown Batch, his face, the crust.
He pulled up every Thursday evening
whistling, 'Oh, believe me if all those endearing

young charms,' then slid out the goods:
wheaten farls, fresh baps, large brown, soda, fadge.
We were the end house on his run, he hoked
into the long drawers with a hooked stick

for the last sliced pan, a Veda well-done
or two squashed iced doughnuts,
'Sure I'll throw those in.' When the others
were in bed and he was gone, I slathered

a scud of butter on a pancake,
sneaked crisps I had put on tick.

The Vegetable Man

was nothing like Willie Scullion,
he was an upside down scallion
with bulging eyes and red hands.
His battered blue van

held trays of freshly dug Queens,
Magilligan carrots, broad beans,
turnips, parsnips, sprouts.
A cigarette in the corner of his mouth,

'I'll gie ye a pound off the lot.'
Forget red peppers, courgettes,
no such thing as a mushroom
in Mosside or Stranocum.

He loaded me with a cardboard box,
flicked me the change from his apron pocket.

The Library Van

There was a carpet in the mobile library
that called to ours every other Tuesday
about four o'clock. We ran to the gate,
clanged up three metal treads into the lull
and smell of books stacked on shelves
from floor to ceiling, with names and words
I longed to know. The north wind rocked the van
as we sat cross-legged, floated out over the Sperrins
to forests in Germany, rabbit holes in England, darkest Peru
and later, to a heath in Yorkshire, the Deep South, The Veld.

I did anything for a book,
read them on the back doorstep
while the kitchen floor was mopped,
took them down fields on sunny days,
curled like a comma on the bed
on rainy holidays in Donegal.
The date stamp and the cardboard ticket
were my passport out, as I scanned for signs
from those who had been before,
turned down a page, left a crumb, a pressed carnation.

Mother's Day

As a boy he was always up first.
One fierce cold day in March

he pulled on a sweater over his pyjamas,
slipped bare feet into plastic boots

and all she saw was the open window,
curtains blowing in an empty room.

He jeuked through the slap in the hedge
into the fields where he knew

frosted grass and dragon's breath,
sheep's wool on barbed wire.

She looked for him
up the brae, at the sheugh,

his name rising
with the curlews.

She was just going for help,
for men to search,

when he dawdled down the lane,
a fistful of primroses,

wild apples in his cheeks,
north wind in his eyes.

Lizzie Remembers the Persian Rug

When the days stretched and air grew warm
we hauled the Persian rug onto the lawn,
birled and tumbled onto its swirls,
free of winter and dark furniture.

Its patterns were our Himalayas,
The Amazon, The Congo Basin.
We traced their secret maps and rivers,
found The Silk Road, jungles, tigers,

helped my mother thump and pound
– once found moth cocoons on the underside –
loosened dust to float with pollen and bees
down the lane, past barns, over the fields.

The carpet aired on bushes until evening,
then we rolled it tight as a new leaf,
hoisted it on our shoulders, the world,
heaved it back to the room where it unfurled

to our bare feet. We lazed and lolled,
lay down on its soft, raised pile.
At night now I replay my mother's freckled arm,
hear the echo in my dreams,

that same definite thwack
to tell me summer's back.

What Would Jesus Say?

We stopped at every hole in the hedge
on the school bus home: Stranocum,
Dervock, *change*, Mosside, the bridge
– The Dry Arch – nearly home.

We stood in the stairwell of the old bone-shaker
stared out at The Arch, our stop looming.
On its one-hundred-year-old stonework
the same tired old paint: *Jesus is Coming.*

One afternoon when we were getting off
as *Jesus is Coming* came up at a lick,
we saw fresh paint and added underneath:
if he rembers to change at Dervock [sic].

Letting it Draw

My father taught me to make tea,
the tea only North Antrim farmers know,
in the dented metal pot where I hoked deep
for swollen leaves to spatter on the china sink.

He hooshed out the pot, took the caddy down
– three spoonfuls of good Indian tea –
then poured the boiling water on,
slapped down the lid, set it on the stove.

We watched and waited
till it drew out into peat liquid
the colour of the Margy in flood.
My mother took hers first –

'Lighthouse tea,' Dad winked, 'blinkin' near water.'
He took his brew stewed, last,
'The spoon could stand up in that.' Two sugars.
I gulped mine with a cloud of milk,

scalded my mouth, thirsty
for promises and clues:
teardrops, dark butterflies and love-hearts
swirling in my cup.

My Father Explains the Universe

'The sun does not actually set,
the moon does not actually rise.'
One evening at the kitchen table
my father plucked a grapefruit from the bowl,

'That is the sun,' he said,
'and that' – holding up a Jaffa orange –
'is the earth.' He held the grapefruit still,
worked the orange round and round,

showed us day and night, winter and summer.
'But why do we not fall off?' we asked.
'And what about the moon?'
He handed me an apple,

I held the moon, saw it wax and wane,
a total eclipse, the pull of the tides.
'There,' he said, taking a bite of the apple,
'it's yours, finish it. I'll have the grapefruit for breakfast.'

Then we put on our coats over our pyjamas
to see The Plough, The Seven Sisters, Orion's Belt.
I never understood how their lights had gone out,
yet we could see them.

'Think of it like this,' he said,
'when someone you love is dead,
they are gone,
but their light shines for years to come.'

New Year's Day

'Keep between the hedges,'
you laughed at the words
you had not heard for years,
then drove off down the lane

to the town for some messages.
The others stayed to clear away the lunch,
fish pie with potatoes and beans,
the big meal you always made

when you were home.
You must have driven out the main line
past the New Year's ploughing match.
They were there from all over

Tyrone, Fermanagh, County Down.
A frost lay on the ground,
the earth was hard,
but old Sammy McCormack

could turn the straightest furrow,
rain, hail or shine.
On your way home it was getting dark
as you stopped in the village

for a cabbage and half a pint of cream.
If you had still lived around here
maybe you would have remembered
the clarry of the dark country road,

the flatbed lorry parked there
no lights.
You kept between the hedges
straight into the back of it.

Muck all over the windscreen,
cabbage and cream all over the car,
you against the steering wheel.
Now the hedges you keep between

are the lines of yew trees
we walked down three days later.
Clay freshly dug, deeper than any furrow,
you cold, stiff as the earth they ploughed.

Offering

For months after the funeral they came
from all over and if we were not about
each left a simple offering at the house,
a bag of spuds set in the porch, no name,
a pheasant, plucked, from the road up the back,
a couple of mackerel, poteen, whiskey,
Madonna and child in a holy picture,
on the windowsill a tin with a big farm brack,
a whole cheese from away down the glen,
a pot of stew still warm on the doorstep.
Between these gifts there was no difference,
left foot or right we were all one in this,
scouring our minds for hope in the face of death,
we hurled prayers into the same sky, same earth.

For the Whole Drive Across Buenos Aires

Coopy held my hand from Hurlingham to Martinez
I sat in the front bench seat of the Zephyr
(he was in the back) it was an awkward angle

my summer dress had broken its strap
only one thin ribbon was holding it up
I had no bra on

I remember wondering what would happen
if the other strap broke
I didn't care

about anything because
the reason he was holding my hand
(even though I hardly knew him)

was that
earlier that afternoon
in the middle of an *asado* party in Buenos Aires

– I was on a swing for the first time
since I was a child
I liked being off the ground

how my feet needed to push air
for height –
in the middle of this party

Richard and Coopy came walking towards me
I waved *hey Richard*
he did not wave back

did not look at me
I stopped swinging
I said *just tell me*

tell me who is dead
quién se ha muerto
tell me

and then I let a big gowl out of me
that travelled the Atlantic
back to Ireland

where they lay in the morgue
where my father had identified them
had made the trunk call

to let Richard know
to let me know
and that's when

he came walking towards me
here the people at the party said
come into this bedroom

the doctor is coming
they crowded round me in a big circle
all the people at the party

in their party clothes
no I said *no doctor*
no quiero médico

yo quiero llorar
yo quiero sentir
esas lágrimas

para nunca sentirlas de vuelta
and the doctor was standing there
with a big needle

I never saw such a big needle
no I said *no quiero*
yes I am crying

it's only normal
and then they all disappeared
(even the doctor)

and there was Richard and me
in the bedroom with built-in wardrobes
lots of mirrors

it was hard to find a way out
I think we went through the French doors
back to the garden where the *asado* was

and into the Zephyr
and that's when Coopy took my hand
– that's when I noticed my dress strap

that I was coming apart –
I felt like I had no clothes on
like I was watching a film with no sound

I don't remember one single thing being said
I don't know how we got from there to here
I don't know how Richard drove

all I know is my hand and arm went numb
so numb it felt like
I had lost my right arm

Open a Wardrobe

Open a wardrobe, she is there,
nothing I can say, or point to.
The smell of mothballs, all
that hangs in the unused air.

Open a handbag, she is there,
old smell of leather long forgotten,
strap perished, white now, rotting.
Golf tee, nail file, half-used lipstick,

perfume spray, half a pack of polo mints.
A wallet with us, her children in it,
a receipt for a watch repair, a theatre ticket.
Only hints.

Forty-eight years have come to this
address book, tissue, shopping list.

Keeping in Touch

Your letter posted in Cloughmills
reaches my P.O. Box in Oxford
and the words on the page are not
from a big farmer walking tall
across fields of clover and cow dung
on a hill farm in the north of Antrim,
not blown by the Atlantic wind
full of gorse and may blossom after the rain.

For years you have written with careful ink
what monks in your school taught you well
– *It will stand you in good stead to know* –
the secret of slipping from one voice to another.
And me over here no better, where I have learned
not only to write but also to speak the bare essentials:
yes please, no thanks, explain scunnered, snib, or sheugh
– but *ditch* does not have the slap and ugh of a sheugh.

The gift of the gab, no, I was not born with it,
but into it, a way of speaking passed down by people
who had to keep their stories in their heads.
Different as chalk on English downs
from the Ulster farmhouse cheese we bought
that day in the glens away up the back road
where fuchsia dangled, self-seeded as our language.

And now I pick at your phrases learned by the sally rod
when my hoarding of home has me craving your voice
basic as buttermilk in wheaten bread,
knowing I must wait until I see you
for words that belong to you, to us:
blaeberries from the mountain
bursting in our mouths.

Just Enough

Just enough of the glow of the street lamp
to see the moon rise above Croagh Hill

just enough of the roar of the cars
to hear the sound of the Atlantic Ocean

just enough of a lorry's horn
to hear the cow in calf

just enough of the passing headlights
to see the sweep of Rathlin's east light at Altacarry

just enough of a walk in the park
to feel the heather on Knockmore Moss

just enough but never enough to stay
just enough but never enough to go back.

Storm Damage
Oxford, 1987

Just before the storm broke
I was out walking the dog
and the Irish man fixing the road said
is that wind strong enough for you
and I laughed and I had no idea

just before the storm broke
I was thinking about six men
I was thinking about Gerry Hunter
John Walker Hugh Callaghan Paddy Hill
Billy Power and Richard McIlkenny and

I had no idea the wind was so strong
because I come from the land where
almost daily you could walk the beach in a Force 10
almost daily the wind would cut right through you
you get used to it

and it was only the radio
I was listening for news of the Birmingham Six or
the three teenagers who raided a betting shop
in West Belfast with toy guns
shot dead or Mandela or Romania

it was only the radio told me
a strong wind blows you better watch out
for your life you never know what might happen
a storm a national alert the radio kept saying
Gale Force 10 and rising and

I had spoken with my friend that same day
him in Belfast me in Oxford
it's blowing a gale I said a national alert
it's a desperate day here too he said
they had the funeral today

and after the storm had passed
I heard a woman and her baby
had sheltered all night under the kitchen table
rain like bullets on the window
and she thought it was the end of the world

and after the storm had passed
I was out walking
trees and car aerials in the gutter
and a man
was walking his dog

the storm was big I said
yes sad very sad he said
about three million trees lost
flattened uprooted destroyed
and I was thinking yes I love trees

and I was thinking yes maybe it is
nearly as sad as The Birmingham Six or
three teenagers who raided a betting shop with toy guns
shot dead nearly as sad
as Mandela or Romania yes nearly

because I come from the land where strong winds blow
everything over almost daily
you better watch out in the middle of
a national alert
you could be blown out the door

crushed almost daily
you could walk out
trees car aerials lying in the gutter
and a man
you get used to it

flattened uprooted destroyed
spend all night under the table
bullets like rain on the window
breaking like the end of the world
and maybe that's just as sad as three million trees

I don't know
I have no idea
I just can't tell from listening to the radio
but I was thinking
maybe it is

The Lump of Ailsa Craig

The shards of limestone
from that last beach walk in Cushendun,

the sea-smoothed beads of black basalt
that I crammed in my jacket pocket

to range on windowsills and mantelpiece
of this damp, rented house in Stratford East

have lost all salt-water lustre
this dreich Tuesday in November

– even the lump of Ailsa Craig
I found shoved in my cabin bag

is a disappearing blue milestone
away from its strand.

I slump at my desk, stare out
at mizzle on pavement,

dark at four o'clock.
I will gather together my sticks,

leave the parched flags, leave all this here:
run for the drenched stones of the shore.

Donegal

The back road

fuchsia hedges
falling away

to the sea

mare's tails
in the big sky

blue smoke
rising
on the mountain.

The Lie of the Land

Your laugh, a curlew's call,
in the back room where we sit
to the small hours.
Stories our mothers told us,

stories, our own,
ramble off, stop
at every last whin bush,
diverge, converge again.

Roddens through the moss,
townlands in our minds,
phrases turn like a sod,
words churn like the butter

we used to know,
as we roll and heuch,
slap rowdy hands on thighs.
Wild she-wolves in native oak groves

we try to find again
the lie of the land,
the different names for different fields,
fallow, meadow, ploughed.

New paths over old tracks,
opening up blocked roads.

Rare Grooves

It is drizzling,
I am driving,
I keep looking at the mountain
and the day,

one of those gorse-against-the-sky,
sunshaft-through-the-rainstorm
(the sort we used to think meant God
parting the clouds with a message),

oh-so-North-Antrim kind of days.
And so anyway, there I am
blaring out my sweet reggae music,
the home-made tape you sent me,

crucial beats, the latest,
serious beats, the classics,
rare grooves, the kind
you go to Jamaica to buy.

The mountain stays with me,
follows me,
so much like the moon
and I think I am Debra Winger

as I drive, I love the way
the May blossom and fuchsia
mark the road in time
with the music,

so much like the film
I'd want to star in.
Well I'm coming to the bad bend
just outside Armoy

and there they are, two of them,
waiting for someone just like me,
a woman alone,
and them not busy,

not many cars
this time of day,
this road.
And so anyway

they stop me,
right in the middle of Black Cinderella,
my favourite track,
and for badness

I keep my music loud.
They are pointing their guns,
I am looking at the mountain,
I screw the window down.

One of them is Scottish,
the other one is black himself,
he wants to check my boot, my bonnet,
the box of groceries in the back seat,

he wants to check my name, address,
where I've come from and where I'm going.
Black Cinderella is still on.
One last question,

he wants to check why
in the wilds of North Antrim
this Irish girl is blasting out
reggae records so rare

even he can't get them.
So I show him the tape,

all the names he wants to see are there.
I tell him you made it and that

you can most likely see
his mother's house
from your front room in Peckham
where he comes from.

He laughs but he keeps pointing his gun.
I wonder what Debra Winger would do.
The Scottish one disnae have a baldy,
but I tell him, dinnae worrae,

on a good day from the mountain
I can see across the sea
to where he comes from.
He laughs

and suddenly we all wonder
where this scenario came from,
so much removed from everything
this stop and search is meant to be,

so much like the film we'd rather star in.
All the words are there, somewhere
between the gun and the mountain,
I look for them,

messages in the sun-shaft,
to give us the script we need to know,
but nothing comes,
so we leave it at that.

I drive on, it is still drizzling,
one of those oh-so-North-Antrim kind of days.
They keep pointing their guns,
I keep looking at the mountain.

Night in Twinbrook

The street lamp through the venetians made us
part of a night-scene as Schubert played us in,
when the helicopter reminded us that this was real
not the dream you spoke of.

There aren't enough hugs in Belfast you said,
so you gave me a Twinbrook special, to make up
for the time we had spent not hugging each other
in the half-light to the sound of rain and tyre marks,
joyriders in an August drizzle who had reached
a dead-end at four a.m.

All night my sleep was full of car lights, curtains blowing,
rain on the scorched road, whirr of machines and people watching us,
you warm beside me breathing out the colours that I know,
as I wondered how to hold on to things I know
when the back field is a new estate
with a made-up name.

Maybe I just needed to hold you,
not to hold on, or out, for a principle I used to believe in
as I tried to slide down memories and touch
years I had missed living over there,
you had lived through here and I had read about
in *The Guardian.*

Maybe it was your touch from somewhere way back
– your eyes as I leaned forward, light on my hair –
that took us to a place before memory
when the spirit moved in the trees,
Irish Oak for thousands of years,
where this all began,

this moment we had waited for
when the dead-end opened,
the field was green again
and things changed before our very eyes.

Jayne Cortez and The Firespitters at the Old Museum

Jayne Cortez and The Firespitters played the Old Museum,
afterwards – not many places open then –
we went for a meal, but where, I don't remember.
Next day I drove her to catch the plane,
her flight was first thing, took the scenic route
over the mountain – murals, views over the city.

We passed the bottom of the Whiterock
up the Glen Road, then a road block, white cordon
– we would have to double back –
a joyrider shot dead early that morning.
We hadn't listened to the radio,
diversion, just go the motorway.

That night a clip on the six o'clock news
showed my golden Vauxhall Astra at the scene
slowing up at the check-point, open windows,
a three-point turn, a query, a frown.
Jayne beside me chanting *Unsubmissive Blues*,
Unsubmissive Blues, yeah, Unsubmissive Blues.

Cycling Home from the Rotterdam Bar

It was a faff to get back from the Rotterdam
– I had my bike so was heading on home –
while the others stood waiting for a taxi
you hopped on behind and took a backie
on my bag rack, legs splayed out while I steered.
Three sheets to the wind we sailed through the back streets,
with a couple of pints in us we were in slo-mo
like under the strobe light at the disco.

So at a check point in May Street, no worries
– even as you swayed behind me on the carrier –
full of Dutch Courage we were invincible,
they waved us on through like a bike was invisible,
then called to our backs just as we disappeared,
'Hey that's dangerous. You've no lights on your rear.'
When over your shoulder you fired back the quip,
'Aye sure, s'ok, for look, my arse lights up.'

Plastic Bullet

As if it is a children's toy for sale
in the local pound shop for say, Age 3+
– contains small parts, may cause choking, not suitable

for infants, British Kitemark – to find tossed
forgotten under the kitchen table
or in a tidy-box to hide the mess.

That Tuesday was just normal,
Anne-Marie went a message, some Marie biscuits
for her Ma and a pint of milk

and don't forget ten Silk-Cut,
keep the change – a Penny Chew for being good –
when it started. She can still feel it.

Blindsided.
Hunkered in the doorway.
Three years just to learn the words

ball, mummy, bye bye
again, or the ones she speaks now, turning
her whole head to see me with her good eye

as we cross the car park in the rain
this Tuesday at the back end of January,
three years to put one foot in front of the other again.

I can hardly keep up with her
sharp as the wind that would skin ye
she tells me her story

she was just fifteen
a three-inch steel plate
where part of her skull used to be

but she just goes on. Nothing else for it.
When I slosh into a puddle in the rain
damp and grit seep in around my foot,

'Aw naw, I've a hole in my boot,' I complain.
'Sure I've a big hole in my head,' she tuts,
'an' ye dinny hear me gurn.'

Getting to Chartres (During Peace Talks Back Home)

We arranged to meet in Chartres
a week Tuesday, the cathedral,
outside on a seat if there was one
– if we miss you then go on
we'll see you in the south or wherever.

We hitched out of Paris on the E50
pitched our tent beside a motorway,
awoke next morning surrounded by cows
– boy, Chartres was hard to get to,
off the main auto-route.

We arrived around lunch
and there you were on a bench
reading a book, expecting us
– our clothes all covered in dust –
you poured half a bottle of Evian

over my dirty, blistered feet.
We ate peaches, cheese, baguettes,
then entered the cool of the apse.
The August sun through the stained glass,
gold, amber, violet,

the rose-window's mosaic
made a walk-through kaleidoscope
into years of emerald, sapphire
projected onto the floor,
your platinum blond hair, a halo.

Maybe it was being suddenly still,
in one place, after all that travel
– land legs again after months at sea –
that and the light, the thirst, the heat,
there was a moment like Stendhal's

when everything stopped, a film with no sound,
we were underwater or high above clouds
all our history washed clean,
as if walking into the mountain.
Onto the top of our heads, a rain

of amethyst light, of blessings, poured in.
Through the open door I heard a pigeon,
a rock dove, call into the middle of the silence,
same note here as its Irish equivalent,
remembered the name *colombe* in French.

She Threw it Right into the Middle of the Garry Bog

as hard as she could,
as far as she could,
into the heather
and newly planted fir trees.

That was twenty years ago
and she can still see it:
stopping the car
on the way to see her boyfriend.

She hadn't told him yet,
but it was the second one
and she was sure this time.
The same unbroken blue line.

She checked it just before
her grandparents arrived to stay
and there it was
as clear as day,

the you I knew
I would never know.
Today she passed there again
for the first time in years,

the trees have grown up so much
it is now called Garry Forest,
hardly any bog left at all,
saplings gone.

Middle Months

I cannot see my feet
let alone reach them,

painting toenails
is too much effort

as my skin tightens
over your growing shape.

Sometimes when I am in bed
at night and all is still,

your hand
pushes me,

sometimes your head,
as you lean against the sides

of this human tent
I have made for you.

Afternoon Mudra

It was the way you tipped handfuls of cowrie shells
you had gathered near Ballycastle
from the velvet drawstring bag onto the kitchen table,
your hand smoothing over them like love, like gold,

the way you spied the beech tree's storm damage,
dragged the fallen branch from the hedge,
wedged it against the car boot to saw into a pile of logs
we burned all night.

And it was you, turning towards me in the glen,
down in the secret place all overgrown
with blackthorn and hazel
where we lay and listened to the waterfall.

It was the blue of your jacket and the red of mine,
as they came together in a currency that we understand.

Crow Glen, Belfast Hills

The waterfall is louder than the helicopter
above us, as my children pick wild carrot, sorrel,
mash it with a stick, make it into soup.
For hours they scrape and peel,
rinse and pound, light imaginary flame
to boil the broth. We find red jasper
under our feet, basalt, limestone, gypsum,
a thousand-year-old flint, as we look through
the hazels at the blue sky of February,
see pollen rise off the catkin, its red flower
that will open to become the nut; unearth
last year's hazelnuts, buried under leaves,
dunk them into the brew. We drink. Wisdom.
This is all there is, all there ever was.

Fine Green Beans

The fine green beans in my steamer
from Kenya, Malawi, Uganda
are the ones
you got up early yesterday
to pick, sort, pack, send
to the factory
to the airport
to the lorry
to the market
to the van
to my local
vegetable shop
where I bought them
this morning.

You have six children
your husband died
of AIDS
you need twenty buckets
of water a day
which your daughters carry
on their heads.

I turn on the tap
to rinse the beans
to cook the dinner
I know my children
won't eat.

They like noodles
from China
tofu from Ashby-de-la-Zouche
but not
fine green beans from Kenya.

My Russian Hat

The African woman carries her shopping
on her head, past My Lady's Road
at the bottom of the Ravenhill.
The doorman from the Czech Republic
points to my Russian hat.
I laugh, he laughs, we talk, no
it is not really funny
for him to see my fashion
statement of his past
where he could not get
any bread
or jeans.

Unmarked

He still has John instead of Séan
on his driving licence
and on nights out
he never wears
the Claddagh ring
his lover gave him.

He still keeps his coat buttoned
on match days
and he wouldn't call out his child's name
in the swimming pool.
He rubs the ashes off his forehead
after early morning mass.

But, now thirty odd years on,
he does swop the neutral white van
for a newly painted one:
'McMullan's Fresh Vegetables,
filled rolls and *baguettes*'
tattooed onto the side.

Flashback
Masserene, 2009

The two soldiers were still on the tarmac
just outside the barracks.
It was raining so hard
the pizza delivery man hunched over the steering wheel,
stuck the van in reverse,
the wipers on double speed,
kept the engine running.
The cardboard box was warm,
a red stain seeped through,
'A margherita and a pepperoni, extra mushroom.'
None of them heard the shots. Pizza all over the road.
Point blank range. It was all over in a second.

It was all over in a second. Point blank range.
None of them heard the shots. Pizza all over the road,
a margherita and a pepperoni, extra mushroom.
A red stain seeped through,
the cardboard box was warm.
The engine kept running,
the wipers on double speed,
the van stuck in reverse,
the pizza delivery man hunched over the steering wheel.
It was raining so hard.
Just outside the barracks
the two soldiers were still, on the tarmac.

Living History

The little bit
of Irish history
he was taught
was a bone sucked dry

all the meat gnawed off.
Sir gave dates, places, names,
chalked titles on the board,
The Famine, Siege of Derry, United Irishmen.

He wanted to stand up
and shout out
Excuse me
would you ever think

of looking out
the window over the city
you can actually see from here
where Henry Joy was hanged,

where Mary Ann lived and worked,
the poorhouse a woman walked to
all the way from Millisle,
twenty miles in search of food?

Can you see the stories
we are making now,
the stones we throw:
Boys' Model/St Gabriel's?

A Musician's Tale

From that day to this
wherever I am
even after I have finished
a concert, in a room
of people, anywhere
there's this constant
movement in my head

that comes from that:

six slaps with the palm
of his hand on the side
of my head,
the pain reaching the very core
of my brain,
he knocked my glasses off,
broke them,

the school teacher.

If he had passed my window
that night
I would have surely killed him
with my father's shot gun –
I had it ready
propped between two pillows –
from the bedroom window.

I was thirteen at the time.

But that night
he did not pass.
Even now
when I look back
I still wish
I had killed him.

If it hadn't been for music –
there is nothing greater.
It changed the chemistry
of my brain.
Yes, it was the music saved me.
It was the cancer killed him in the end.

Departure Lounge Heathrow to Belfast

– Aye, haven't been over
in thirty years,

just back for a few days
then that's me away.

I left, no option.
Got out. Best thing.

Don't miss it at all,
naw

only going over to bury
me ma –

his jeans stick up
in an awkward shape

where his knee-
cap used to be.

Café

– You're effin' nuts –
he said to me
that day in the café
as we sat holding hands,
not,
after that.

After that
I still stayed on, latte with hazelnut
syrup, my stomach in knots,
as he laid into me,
said I was underhand,
right there in the café.

As I sipped my café
con leche, he said that
he was washing his hands,
that I was just effin' nuts,
it was to do with me
and he was not

to blame. Absolutely not.
I should wake up and smell the coffee.
Always me, me, me,
and that was that,
in a nutshell.
I might as well raise my hands

now. But he would hand
it to me, at least I was not
as much of a fruit-and-nutcase
as that other caffeine-head
and that
was saying something. Even for me.

Then here's me:
I grabbed his hand,
I said that
I did not
want him to pay for my coffee,
even though it cost peanuts,

nut that I was, I could handle
that particular cappuccino; I did not stay
and took my *café noisette* with me.

Daylighgin

Looking back maybe it was already broken
even then, or maybe we were just knackered

after so many sleepless nights, hectic days,
work, children, running a house

or just running
whichever way, my cousin

kept the children
– a night to yourselves

sure you'd like that – she laughed
but to tell you the truth

the house felt empty, echoes,
dents in cushions, unfilled shoes

on the stairs
still, it was good to have a breather

we opened a bottle of Chardonnay
went to bed early

awoke at 3am to a crash
took a while to realise

a hood was bashing a boulder
taken from our neighbour's

newly landscaped front garden,
not only that, but even

as you opened the window to shout – *Stop* –
he lifted the big blue flower pot

Ursula had given us
planted with special black tulips

from Amsterdam, then took a second,
even a third, run

at our triple-glazed front door.
It's the Beamer. He's after the Beamer,

you said, *it's parked outside.*
I was a leaf in the wind

it wasn't even our car
but your city brain clocked it right there.

The neighbours came, police came,
a bizarre pyjama party in our front room.

Phil made us a cup of tea
(thank goodness the house is tidy

I stupidly thought) the stained glass rose
was shattered to pieces

the door completely banjaxed.
We taped and swept next day

you re-drew the rose for the glaziers
rang the insurers

not really worth it to be honest
ended up costing us –

the year after we put the claim in
they slapped on a huge premium –

either way within a few years
lovely Ursula was dead, a sudden tumour,

we were in smithereens ourselves
and I closed in on myself

like a black tulip's crown
when the daylight is gone.

I Text Myself Before Bedtime

I text myself before bedtime
just to see *one message received,*
and phone myself
to have *one missed call.*

I sleep in my clothes,
haven't showered for a week
so I can smell myself on myself
and know I am here.

I cram yoghurt, oatcakes, nuts,
anything to fill me up.
I still can't get the measure
of porridge for one.

It is hard to keep on going,
but it keeps on going anyway.
The dishes are still in the sink.
So much food goes to waste.

My dad told me to freeze the bread,
take out one slice at a time.
In the evening everything is exactly the way I left it
in the morning, no dinner on, no fire.

Sometimes I turn on the lights, the radio, the heat,
then drive away again for ten minutes,
come back to my own welcome
and hope for the smell of onions cooking

through next door's wall.
Sometimes I wake in the middle of the night
to the sound of the ocean,
the unused pillow beside me, full

of thoughts like *could* or *should have been*.
But. If. Only. Small words that open out
like those scrunch T-shirts. Endless.
One cold snap in November

I dragged the dog into bed,
wedged its back against mine,
just to feel another breathe beside me,
the rise and fall in perfect time.

Eóin's Last Day at School

I remember his first
            do you
                    of course I do
                            the years have flown

a swift
        rising
                on cushions of air
                        he flies

into his own summer
                    May, his month
                            when grasses flower
                                        hawthorn blossoms

ferns unfurl
        chestnuts flame
                even the stubborn ash
                            admits the summer.

The Eel on the Farm

My father caught an eel one day on the farm
– years ago when there was still a stream
ran over the old coach road beside the inn;
he played there after school, threw sticks, built dams,
caught sticklebacks, newts, freshwater shrimp –
he knew if he trapped the critter with his bare hands
it could slide through his fingers to nothing.

It slithered over the fields to the sheugh
so he found the dredging fork – used to clear scutch –
hooked it between the prongs in one deft flick
then hoiked it up into the old Belfast sink
the cattle drank from. No harm done.
He kept it there a week, studied it after class
each day, hunkered over, mesmerised,

as he stared he swears it returned his gaze.
The odd memory can get a bit hazy,
slips through the net, does not come,
while this one holds, will not let go of him.

Seasoned

He cannot bend to tie his shoe.
I stoop to make the knot
that takes me back
to when he carried fully grown men
down stairs in the middle of the night,

found them in floods or snowdrifts,
hauled them up cliffs on stretchers,
pulled them out of sheughs and bogs,
'all in a day's work,'

he held mothers' hands in ambulances,
gave the kiss of life
in porches, on roadsides,
delivered babies in toilets
of country bars long after closing.

At home he bathed us on a Saturday night,
bent over the tub, sleeves rolled up,
arms covered in suds,
told stories of him as a boy
when once he cycled twenty miles to run a race
and won, then cycled twenty home.

His back, a solid Irish oak,
bent, moved, straightened
to each particular need.
Now its knots tell the years
of a thousand people who leant on him,
shoulders that carried other people's lives
as well as his own.

He cannot bend to tie his shoe
and I have learned to make the loop.

Snowfall

for Andrew

Thinking about my mother, how
she always cooked with her coat on,

straight in the door,
chopped and sweated the onion,

or in the garden, how she knelt
on an old hot water bottle

to plant crocus, daffodils, snowdrops;
how I'm older now than she was

when she died that January day
on the way home from town,

as the light was fading
on a quiet country road.

My little brother was watching cartoons
when my father told him

that she had died in his arms,
there was nothing he could do.

There were so many words
that would not come,

just snow that settled
all that week before the funeral

when the cold cut like a knife
and everything was frozen.

Road, Glen, Island, Ocean

Sometimes she was stuck on the other side
of the road, opposite the tennis courts,
the cars bumper to bumper on a July day.
We spoke across the shimmer of fumes and heat.

Or she was walking down into the glen,
through moss, wet grass, as the late August sun
filtered through the hazels, picking out midges
and the thread of her hair.

Once, on an island, she climbed on ahead
to a rocky outcrop, for the view. I scrambled up
through gorse and bracken, but the last boat
was leaving and I had to go.

The last time was on the long sweep of the strand
near our house. She was wearing that pink shirt-dress
with earrings, like sweets, to match.
The Atlantic wind lit her eyes as she turned from me

and waded into the rollers, clothes and all.
I kept my eye on her, but what with the waves
and the sunlight fizzing off the water,
it got harder to make out what was her

and what was not, until she was just another dot
in all the shining dots that make up light.

Old Croagh Woman

And some day you will find her,
not with her arms pierced
with hazel stakes, a sacrifice,
head severed where they bound her,

but in full lotus position
at the bottom of the bog,
centuries snug,
not far from this rodden

where she died,
legs crossed,
eyes half-closed,
palms to the sky,

sunk deep in bog fir,
where she bundled hazel, willow,
wove herself a bracken pillow,
climbed aboard the floating pyre;

and when you find her,
carve one like her into bog-oak,
take her to the top of Croagh
and write: she lived, she loved, she died.

Rushes, Port na Cailleach on St Brigid's Day

I grow in the meadow field
where land gives way
to the Atlantic.

Salt wind and boggy ground
make me who I am,
North Antrim

basalt holds me
beyond reason.
When I find myself

in your house I know
my day has come.
I have been waiting

for your hands,
your fingers work me,
I fold, open

into the shape
I was always meant to be,
three-times fire goddess:

the first catkin, a word, a sign.

Walking to Marconi's

At first I think it is seaweed,
the brown band that stretches from the shore
about half-way out to the island

all along the sweep of the beach
and on, to the headland.
Then I see it is the water from the river,

high with run-off from the storm,
churned up mud and peat
that came sliding down from the mountain

into the glen, made its way to the sea.
The stained waves hurl giant suds,
I know there is deeper green beyond.

The car door nearly blows off its hinges
as I step into the bluster of early October.
It is more like itself now.

It is the noise of the sea.
How could I have lived so long away
from the sound of it against the rocks

on one side, the chime of water down the hill
on the other, so long without
these broad flat blades of grass

that hold a single drop of rain?
I walk round to Marconi's
as fuchsia hedges spill onto the verge,

blackberries almost over,
first hazels in the scrub above
where we used to go for the scrog.

I count the beats between
the looms of the East Light,
wait for it to come round again

and again.
Then there is this bit of road
where the wall ends

and there is only air
between me and ocean.
Almost at Marconi's,

when long low clouds
gather over the sound.
I turn around

and reach the car
just as the island disappears
and the heavens open.

NOTES

'Storm Damage': The Birmingham Six were wrongfully sentenced to life imprisonment in 1975 for crimes which they did not commit. Their convictions were quashed in 1991 when they were released after nearly 17 years in prison.

In 'Jayne Cortez and The Firespitters at the Old Museum': *Unsubmissive Blues* (*Bola Press, 1980*) is the title of an album by Jayne Cortez, the jazz blues poet who died in 2012.

'Plastic Bullet': 14 people, half of them children, were killed by plastic bullets in Northern Ireland between 1974 and 1996, many more sustained serious injuries. This poem is dedicated to Ann Marie Loughran.

'She Threw it Right into the Middle of the Garry Bog': This is spoken by the main character, Ailsa, in *The Full Stop Monologues* for which I gratefully received a SIAP Drama Award from the Arts Council of Northern Ireland, 2014.

'Old Croagh Woman' is dedicated to all those disappeared. It was inspired by the television programme *The Bog Bodies* ©BBC 2006, director John Hayes-Fisher, about the discovery of Old Croghan Man. It was also inspired by Seamus Heaney's Bog poems and the first line echoes 'Tollund Man'. His poem 'Blackberry-Picking' also inspired 'After Blackberry-Picking'.

In 'For the Whole Drive Across Buenos Aires':
asado: barbecue.
quién se ha muerto: who is dead
no llores: do not cry.
yo quiero llorar: I want to cry.
quiero sentir esas lágrimas para nunca sentirlas de vuelta: I want to feel these tears so that I never have to feel them again.

The following will be known by people familiar with the words of North Antrim, some of which are also used in other parts of Ireland and Scotland:

birled: turned round and round
clarry: muck
critter: creature
croagh : means hill in Irish
daylighgin: twilight
dinny/dinnae: don't
disnae have a baldy: hasn't a clue
dreich: gloomy, miserable
gowl: howl, roar, shout
gurn: complain, whine
heuch: laugh
hoiked: lifted up swiftly
hoked: rummaged
hooshed: rinsed
hunkered: knelt, squatted
jeuked: ducked
moss: bog
rodden: road through the bog
scrog: gathering hazelnuts
scud of butter: a wedge of butter
scunnered: fed up
sheugh: ditch
slap in the hedge: a gap in the hedge

ELAINE GASTON is from the north coast of Ireland. She received an ACE Award from the Arts Council of Northern Ireland 2014-15. She was awarded the No Alibi's Prize at the Seamus Heaney Centre for Poetry, Queen's University, Belfast, where she completed an M.A. in 2010. She won a Commendation in the National Poetry Competition, 2013, a Special Commendation in the Patrick Kavanagh Award in both 2013 and 2014 and was short-listed for the Bridport Prize in 2014. She has also won prizes in the Templar Poetry Pamphlet Competition and the Academi Cardiff International Poetry Competition. Her work was selected for Poetry Ireland Introductions, 2006.

'Push-Bike' was also commissioned as a film-poem by the Poetry Society, directed by Robert Peake. It premiered in 2014 at the Antwerp Filmpoem Festival and in the UK at the Poetry International Festival at the Southbank, London.